DATE DUE			

FIGHTING SHIPS

U-BOAT

Richard Humble

Franklin Watts
New York · London · Toronto · Sydney

© Franklin Watts 1990

First published in the
United States by
Franklin Watts Inc.
387 Park Avenue South
New York, NY 10016

Photograph credits
Imperial War Museum
13T, 13B, 18, 23B,
27; Popperfoto 5,
15, 16, 21, 23T;
Suddeutscher Verlag 7;
Ullstein 6, 8, 9T, 9B, 10.

Designer: Ben White
Picture researcher:
Sarah Ridley
Illustrations: Doug Harker,
Peter Chesterton
Maps: Hayward Art Group

Printed in Belgium

Library of Congress Cataloging-in-Publication Data
Humble, Richard.
   U-boat/by Richard Humble.
      p. cm.—(Fighting ships)
   Includes index.
   Summary: A brief history of German submarine warfare during World
War II and the measures taken by the Allies to combat the U-boats.
   ISBN 0-531-14023-7
   1. World War, 1939-1945—Naval operations—Submarine—Juvenile
literature. 2. World War, 1939-1945—Naval operations, German—
Juvenile literature. 3. World War, 1939-1945—Campaigns—Atlantic
Ocean — Juvenile literature. 4. Submarine boats—Juvenile literature. [1.
World War, 1939-1945—Naval operations — Submarine. 2. World War,
1939-1945—Campaigns — Atlantic Ocean. 3. Submarine boats.] I. Title.
II. Series.
D781.H86 1990
940.54'51—dc20   89-35888
                                                                           CIP
                                                                            AC

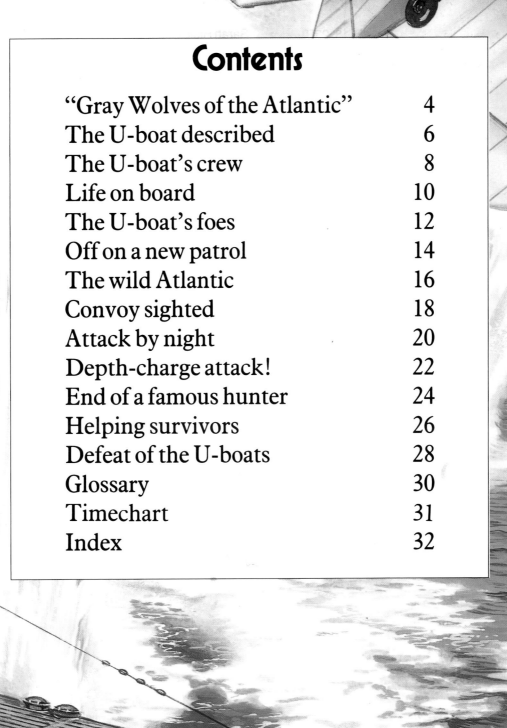

Contents

"Gray Wolves of the Atlantic"

The U-boat – short for *Unterseeboot*, the German word for "submarine" – was Germany's most dangerous weapon in both World Wars. The U-boat was the supreme unseen peril. It would strike from beneath the waves by day and night, using its **torpedoes** to sink the merchant ships carrying the weapons, supplies, and food without which Britain and the United States could not have won the war.

In World War II the "Battle of the Atlantic" against the U-boats lasted for the length of the war: from September 1939 to May 1945. Its most desperate months, however, were those between the summer of 1940 and the spring of 1943. The purpose of the U-boats was to sink so many merchant ships that the United States would be unable to supply Britain by sea. The aim of Britain and the United States was to sink more U-boats than

Germany could replace. It was a deadly battle, measured by the efforts of brave men and gallant ships on both sides.

The U-boats of World War II had an enormous advantage over those on patrol in 1914–1918. In World War I, Germany's U-boats had to sail around the British Isles before they could attack the **convoys** of merchant ships crossing the Atlantic. But after Germany had conquered both Norway and France in 1940, U-boats could be based on ports in both countries, on either side of Britain. This advantage cut hundreds of miles off the distance from Germany to the Atlantic, extending the time in which U-boats could prowl the seas before heading home for more fuel, food, and weapons. Once Germany had built enough U-boats, their **wolf packs** could strike at will.

▷ Early morning, and as the sun rises a group of U-boats heads out to sea for its next patrol, hunting for merchant ship convoys in the Atlantic Ocean.

▷ A U-boat in the North Sea, running on the surface under the power of its diesel engines. The rows of holes in the outer casing help seawater to flow rapidly in when the ballast tanks are flooded to dive, and out again when the tanks are blown empty to surface. The fact that this U-boat is not crash-diving proves that the picture was taken from a German aircraft!

The U-boat described

Between 1935 and 1945 Nazi Germany produced 26 different types of U-boat, but the most successful in the Battle of the Atlantic was the Type VIIC.

Like all submarines, the Type VIIC consisted of an inner **pressure hull** containing the engines, living quarters, **control room**, and the working areas where the torpedo tubes were loaded and fired. The pressure hull was surrounded by an outer envelope of **ballast tanks** which were flooded with seawater to dive, and blown empty with compressed air to surface.

The U-boat's main weapons were its torpedo tubes. The Type VIIC carried five, four in the bow and one in the stern. A Type VIIC carried 14 torpedoes and a

△ In the late 1930s, new U-boats lie waiting for their crews, who are paraded on the dockside in their best uniforms. These are small, coastal boats known as Type IIs.

▽ The batteries for the electric motors were stowed in the lowest level of the pressure hull, close to the spare torpedoes.

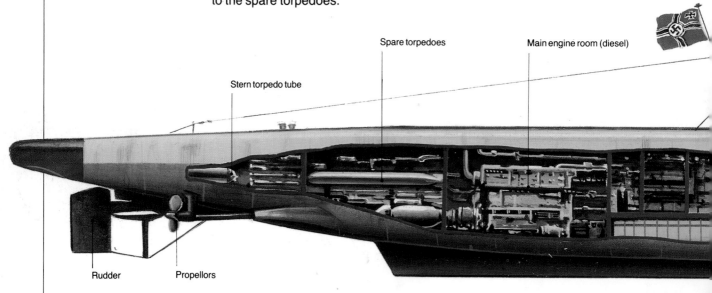

Spare torpedoes

Main engine room (diesel)

Stern torpedo tube

Rudder   Propellors

▷ In an armored "U-boat pen" on the French Atlantic coast, a crew returns to a U-boat which has been repaired after suffering damage on its last patrol.

wise U-boat captain never wasted one. The other weapon was the 88 mm deck gun, used to sink ships in attacks on the surface.

Like a whale, a U-boat had to rise to the surface at regular intervals. This was not only to renew the air, but also to use the diesel engines to recharge the batteries of the electric motors on which the U-boat ran when submerged.

◁ When making attacks on enemy shipping, the main periscope was lowered and a shorter, less-revealing "attack periscope" (to the left of the main periscope) was used.

Periscopes

Control room

Deck gun

Spare torpedoes

Bow torpedo tubes

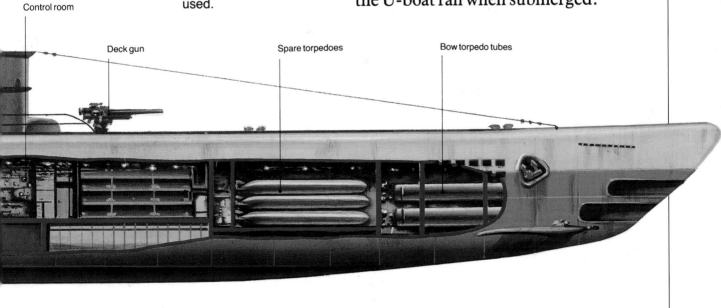

The U-boat's crew

The crew of a Type VIIC U-boat was 44 officers and men. Like all submarine crews they had to learn to live and work together in conditions that were always cramped, damp with condensation and dirty, especially by the end of a long ocean patrol. Water on board was mainly for drinking and cooking, and most U-boat men came home from patrol with generous growths of unshaven beard.

U-boat crewmen were issued with a wide variety of kit, from oilskins as protection against rough weather to red

▷ Seagoing rig for Captain and crewman.
▽ This view of U-boat crewmen, paraded on the upper casing for an inspection by their flotilla commander, gives a good idea of the seagoing kit worn by U-boat men.

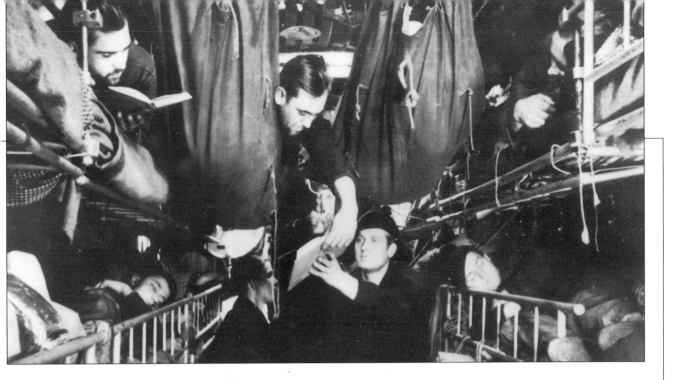

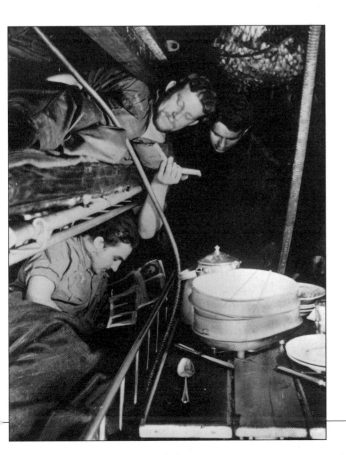

△ U-boat crewmen relax off watch. For most – as in nearly every navy – the main attraction was "getting your head down," or sleeping. Others would prefer to read, play cards, or maybe write letters in their very cramped quarters.

▽ In the "fore ends" or bow compartment of the U-boat, off-watch crewmen ate and slept close alongside the ship's torpedo tubes and the torpedoes stacked ready for loading and firing in action.

eye glasses to accustom the eyes when going on deck at night (see page 10). But uniform rules were never strict. U-boat life made it impossible to keep clothes clean for long, and the men tended to wear what was most suitable for their jobs. In the heat of the engine room, for example, shorts were always more popular than pants and men often stripped to the waist to work.

One of the most important duties on board a U-boat was that of the lookouts. In conditions ranging from the terrifying fury of Atlantic gales to calm seas and blazing sunshine, it was the lookouts who, with their excellent Zeiss binoculars, searched the horizon for the funnel smoke of their victims. They kept constant watch for the British and American aircraft and warships which could be their death.

It was a world of steel and artificial light. Sailors in surface warships are never far from a glimpse of daylight, but U-boat crewmen often had to live by electric light for days at a time, with only the clock to tell them the time of day.

Life on board

Life aboard a U-boat was not for the faint-hearted. It was cramped, tough, and as each patrol wore on, it became increasingly dirty. There was neither room nor water to spare for baths.

U-boat crewmen learned to live and work efficiently in confined spaces. Every man had his working space, and when the boat was submerged uncontrolled movement was strictly forbidden because of the need to preserve the submarine's balance – known as the "trim."

One very obvious problem was that there was only one bathroom for the whole crew, which only one man could use at a time. A red light showed when it was in use, and for many anxious U-boat crewmen that red light seemed to shine forever!

The men slept on folding beds fitted to the walls or bulkheads in their working areas – even in the torpedo rooms at either end of the boat.

The periods when a U-boat surfaced to recharge its batteries and the boat could be ventilated with fresh sea air were all too brief. When the U-boat was submerged, dampness and condensation tended to make bread go moldy, food cans rust, and the men suffer from headaches and skin complaints.

The time most favored for the vital battery charge was at night, when there was less chance of being sighted. To adjust the men's eyes from electric lighting inside to the darkness outside, U-boat crewmen going on watch had to wear red-tinted eye glasses.

On a long Atlantic patrol, one of the most important men on board was the cook. His skill at getting the most out of the boat's rations was of the greatest importance in keeping the men fit and cheerful. U-boat crews longed to capture refrigerated, food-carrying merchant ships whose cargos were filled with delicious fresh meat, eggs, fruit, and vegetables – but such prizes of war were rare.

◁ Freezing conditions for the officer of the watch and lookouts of a U-boat in Arctic waters. As in the Atlantic, U-boats proved one of the deadliest weapons in attacks on British and American convoys carrying supplies to North Russia, often in appalling, hurricane weather.

▷ "Enemy in sight!" Crewmen rush to their diving stations as the ballast tanks are flooded and the diesel engines shut down for an emergency dive. Last man down into the control room, the Captain whirls shut the conning tower hatch, sealing the pressure hull.

The U-boat's foes

In World War II, U-boats faced a wider range of enemies than they had in 1914–18. There were long-range patrol aircraft capable of spotting a U-boat hundreds of miles out at sea. They could attack with bombs, gunfire and **depth-charges**, which could be set to explode at different depths. These aircraft could also send radio messages to help nearby surface warships join in the hunt, and could be fitted with powerful searchlights – **Leigh lights** – to spot U-boats on the surface at night.

Warships hunting for U-boats used **sonar** (**asdic** to the British) to detect U-boats under water. In the early months of

▷ Look-outs scan the horizon through their binoculars. No matter how tired they are, the safety of all on board depends on them.

12

World War II, the only weapon was the depth-charge, but later warships were fitted with mortars (known as **Hedgehog** and **Squid**). These fired a number of bombs which hit the water in a wide cluster, each exploding on contact with a U-boat.

A later aid in hunting for U-boats was "narrow beam" radar, which could find even the small target of a submarine on the surface. There was also a high frequency direction finder (HF/DF), which could determine a U-boat's position from the radio signals it sent. Once this was known, the hunting warships could close in and launch accurate attacks on the U-boat.

A U-boat on patrol needed constant alertness to survive all these threats. When running on the surface, lookouts constantly scanned the horizon and the sky. In cloudy or foggy weather they used their ears too, listening for the sound of aircraft engines. No U-boat captain preparing to surface would ever do so before making a thorough search of both the horizon and the sky through the **periscope**.

△ "River" class frigate, a type of warship specially designed for hunting down and destroying U-boats. Unlike the slower corvettes, they could steam faster than a surfaced U-boat.

◁ The old British destroyer *Viscount* has located a U-boat in the North Sea, and has already made one attack with its depth-charges. Now the depth-charge party hastily prepares fresh charges before making the next attack.

13

Off on a new patrol

The Battle of the Atlantic would have been over far sooner if both sides had used their bomber aircraft properly. If the German Air Force had lent long-range aircraft to the German Navy instead of using them to bomb British cities, the U-boats would have been greatly helped in finding convoys to attack far out at sea. But Reich Marshal Hermann Göring, head of the German Air Force, boasted that "Everything that flies belongs to me!" and refused to help the German Navy.

The British made their mistakes, too. A major British error was to use Royal Air Force bombers only to attack factories in Germany and German surface warships in port. This left the Germans free to build huge, protected U-boat bases – known as **pens** – in the sea ports they had conquered on the Atlantic coast of France: Lorient, St. Nazaire, Brest, La Pallice, and Bordeaux.

These pens gave U-boats all the safety they needed to make repairs and take on fuel, food, water and more torpedoes, between patrols. Covered with layers of

concrete up to 7 meters (24 feet) thick, the pens were bomb-proof.

When British and American bombers finally started to attack the U-boat pens, in late 1942 and 1943, it was too late. Although thousands of tons of bombs were dropped on them, no U-boat was ever destroyed in one of the U-boat pens.

Always eager to give the idea that Germany's warships could come and go as they pleased, German news films always made much of U-boats returning from sea or setting out on a new patrol. The U-boats were played in and out of port by military bands; often the crew, lined up on parade on the U-boat's upper casing, would be saluted as it passed by senior officers. These included Grand Admiral Erich Raeder, commander of the German Navy; and Admiral Karl Dönitz, commander of the Navy's U-boat fleet, who took over the Navy from Raeder in early 1943.

These, then, were the formidable bases from which ever-growing numbers of U-boats sailed to join the Battle of the Atlantic in 1942 and 1943.

◁ Overhauled, refueled, rearmed, and stocked with fresh provisions, a U-boat leaves its pen for another Atlantic patrol, played out to sea by stirring tunes by a military band.

△ Leaning over their conning tower rails, officers and men of two U-boats exchange news and experiences during a meeting in the safe waters of their home base.

The wild Atlantic

The wild storms of the North Atlantic, with their hurricane-strength winds churning the sea into giant waves and tearing breakers, were a constant nightmare both for the merchant ship convoys and the U-boats which hunted them.

An Atlantic storm made it almost impossible for the ships of a convoy to keep the close formation that was their best protection. The aftermath of a storm was a moment of great danger for a convoy, as the escort warships scattered to round up "stragglers" – ships which had lost contact with the convoy during the storm. But conditions in a surfaced U-boat were appalling, with the submarine pitching wildly on the giant waves which swept it from bow to stern. The only comfort in these conditions was that they were just as bad for the enemy, who would have little chance to attack.

When on the surface during a storm, the U-boat's lookouts had to lash themselves to the **conning tower** rail with belts to stop themselves being swept overboard. Despite their protective leather clothing, oilskins, and sou'wester hats, they would come off watch soaked to the skin by driving spray, rain and hail. In such conditions, getting a navigating **fix** from the sun or a star was immensely difficult – yet vital for the safety of the U-boat and the success of its mission.

In one such storm, a giant breaker washed the captain of *U–325* overboard at the moment he came out on to the conning tower, before he had had the chance to secure himself. He was picked up by brilliant seamanship after only six minutes in the water – but he had had to abandon his leather jacket, pants, boots, gloves, binoculars and sextant to keep himself afloat.

◁ Another day begins for an Atlantic convoy, viewed from the bridge of an escorting battleship. It shows the wide expanse of sea taken up by a convoy; the outer escort warships are not even in sight.

▷ In rough Atlantic weather, low clouds make it impossible for a U-boat Captain to take a noon sight of the sun through the sextant. "Pack attacks" on convoys were impossible to make unless each U-boat could report its exact position at sea from day to day.

Convoy sighted

The sight most eagerly desired by a U-boat's lookout was the masts and funnel smoke on the distant horizon which marked a convoy: the long-awaited prey.

Here was the chance of sinking the biggest number of ships and their vital war cargos – food, oil, petrol, weapons, and ammunition – on which the Allies depended for victory.

A U-boat sighting a convoy would try to remain on the surface for as long as possible, for two reasons. First, a U-boat's diesel engines could deliver a surface speed of 16 knots – often faster than that of the convoy, which had to steam at the speed of its slowest ship. This speed advantage helped the U-boat to get into the best possible position from which to launch an attack.

As the German signals flashed back and forth the men in the U-boats knew that their messages were being listened to by the British Admiralty, which would warn the convoy and its escorts that there were U-boats in the area. But until the British fitted their ships with the high frequency direction finder – HF/DF, known as "Huffduff" – it was impossible for them to discover a signaling U-boat's actual

△ A convoy seen from the air, zig-zagging from side to side to make it harder for U-boats to attack.

▷ Two U-boats prepare to dive, having sighted the telltale massed funnel smoke of a convoy on the horizon.

position. The first successful trial of "Huffduff" was not made until summer 1941, and over a year passed before the device could be fitted in American ships.

As nightfall approached, the gathering wolf pack prepared to close in and attack under cover of darkness.

The second reason for remaining surfaced was the more important one. The first U-boat to sight a convoy would immediately send a radio report to the U-boat headquarters at Kerneval, near Lorient in north-west France. From Kerneval, Admiral Dönitz and his staff would signal to all U-boats in the area, giving the convoy's position and ordering them to steer toward it. This was the process known as the "forming of the wolf pack," the gathering together of as many U-boats as possible, hopefully to launch so many attacks on the convoy that its escorting warships would not be able to cope.

Attack by night

The deadliest U-boat attacks on British convoys were made in the opening months of World War II's second year: the autumn of 1940. This period was remembered by the U-boat fleet as the "Happy Time," and with good reason. In July 1940, U-boats managed to sink 38 ships (total 195,825 tons). In August this figure jumped to 56 ships, in September 59, and in October 63 (total 352,407 tons). By the end of October, for every U-boat which the British managed to sink, the others were sinking 930 tons of merchant shipping *every day* – a rate of destruction which the U-boat fleet was never to match for the rest of the war.

The reasons for the "Happy Time" were simple. The convoys being attacked only had a handful of escorting warships for defense against the U-boats – often three or less. Though U-boat numbers were small (there were never more than eight or nine of them operating in the Atlantic at a time), they were attacking far beyond the furthest range at which most convoys could be properly escorted. This, of course, was thanks to the new U-boat bases on the French coast. Nor had any of the new technology of later years – the Leigh light, "Huffduff," or the narrowbeam radar – yet been developed by the British.

But the real reason for the "Happy Time" of the U-boats was the simple but effective tactics used by the most expert U-boat commanders: the "aces." They had realized that sonar, the only British method of locating submarines, only

△ A torpedoed merchant ship erupts in flame as another U-boat surfaces between the lines of merchant ships. From here, in the heart of the convoy, it was easy to score hits.

△ An American oil tanker blazing after being hit by a U-boat's torpedo. Though it is hard to believe, the very gallant crew managed to beat the flames and bring their ship to port.

worked against *submerged* ones: it was useless against submarines that remained on the surface, and on a moonless night a surfaced submarine was practically impossible to see. The top-scoring U-boat aces – three of the most famous of whom were Günther Prien (*U–47*), Joachim Schepke (*U–100*) and Otto Kretschmer (*U–99*) – therefore preferred night attacks on the surface. To make their attacks even more deadly, they would work their way *inside* the convoy, between the lines of merchant ships, where it was almost impossible to miss.

On the surface, too, the U-boats had the advantage of the greater speed of their diesel engines, often more than that of the warships hunting them.

The most effective attacks of the "Happy Time" took place between October 16-20 1940. The victims were two convoys approaching each other in mid-Atlantic, which were repeatedly attacked by a "wolf pack" of six U-boats. Over those four dreadful nights, one convoy lost 17 cargo ships and tankers out of 34, the other lost 14 out of 49, while four other ships were damaged. With more U-boats at sea in 1940, the Germans could have won the war in six months.

Depth-charge attack!

If an attacking U-boat was spotted by an escort warship, and had no chance of escaping under cover of darkness, its only chance was to crash-dive and hope to escape the sonar of its attacker.

A U-boat captain had several ways of doing this. He could dive deep, beyond sonar range. He could order "silent routine:" total silence with engines switched off, to avoid detection by enemy **hydrophones.** Otherwise he could release a "pill" of chemicals which boiled furiously in the U-boat's wake. This formed a dense patch of seething bubbles which sonar could detect – like a scared octopus squirting a cloud of ink to fool an enemy.

Everything, however, depended on how experienced an enemy the U-boat had up above, and how good its sonar operator was. An experienced sonar operator could tell the difference between the bubble-patch of a "pill" and the more solid sound

▽ Too close for comfort – the shattering explosion of a depth-charge savagely shakes a U-boat during an attack, causing leaks and broken glass dials demanding prompt repair.

△ A depth-charge on its thrower, ready for firing over the suspected position of the U-boat.

▽ Seen from the attacking destroyer, an exploding depth-charge hurls up a mountain of water.

reflected by a U-boat. An expert U-boat hunter would guess which way the U-boat captain would choose to go, and out-turn him before closing in to attack with depth-charges. For his part, the U-boat captain under attack would try to out-guess and out-turn the warships hunting him, and therefore slip clear of the hunting warships' sonar.

All U-boat men dreaded the depth-charge, which the Germans called *wasserbomb* – "water-bomb." Inside the U-boat it was often possible to hear the *"chuff-chuff-chuff"* of the attacking warship's propellers passing overhead. There would be a nerve-racking pause – then the shattering roar of the exploding depth-charges, shaking the U-boat like a violent storm. Glass dials would shatter, men would be hurled off their feet, and water spurted in from a dozen leaks. Even a close near-miss from a depth-charge could cause so much damage that the only chance was to blow all ballast tanks, rise to the surface, and hope to fight it out gun to gun.

End of a famous hunter

By the end of 1940 the "Happy Time" of the U-boats was already drawing to a close, as the British sent more and more escort warships out to defend the convoys. They were greatly helped by the transfer of 50 old destroyers, no longer needed by the American navy, from the United States to Britain. The long and painful experience of 16 months of U-boat hunting was producing a new force in the Battle of the Atlantic: surface escort U-boat hunters, with skills equal to those of the U-boat aces.

Then came the amazing month of March 1941: the first major setback for the U-boat fleet, with two aces killed and one

captured within 10 days. First to go was Günther Prien of *U–47*, sunk in company with *U–70* while attacking a convoy on March 17. Ten days later it was the turn of Joachim Schepke of *U–100* and Otto Kretschmer of *U–99*, and their different fates show the growing pressures on the top U-boat commanders by the spring of 1941.

Schepke and Kretschmer had joined forces to attack Convoy HX.112, heading for Britain from Halifax in Canada. Both U-boats were sighted on the surface by destroyers which did not waste a minute in attacking. The destroyer *Vanoc* sighted the wake of *U–100* at very close range – so close that *Vanoc* rammed and sank the U-boat, killing Schepke on his conning tower in the collision.

Worn out by days without enough sleep, Kretschmer was taking a nap when *U–99* was sighted by the destroyer *Walker*. Instead of trying to escape on the surface, the officer commanding *U–99* made the decision to dive. It was a fatal mistake. The U-boat was immediately detected by *Walker*'s sonar and an accurate depth-charge attack left *U–99* so badly damaged that there was no choice but to surface and surrender.

Kretschmer's capture was a great relief to the British. He was the top-scoring U-boat ace of World War II, having sunk 44 merchant ships (total 266,629 tons) and one destroyer.

U–99's badge, carried on the conning tower, was a golden horseshoe with the points down. "Well," said the British captain when Kretschmer came aboard *Walker*, "with your horseshoe upside down, your luck was bound to run out!"

◁ The night of March 17 1941, and the luck finally runs out of the upside-down "Golden Horseshoe" on *U-99*'s conning tower. The stricken U-boat surfaces for the last time, her crew preparing to sink her before surrendering to the British destroyer *Walker*.

Helping survivors

To their victims – the men in the merchant ships which were their prey – the U-boats were the most dreaded menace of World War II: the pitiless threat which lurked unseen and could strike at any hour of the day or night.

When U-boats attacked merchant ships sailing in defended convoys, there was little they could do to care for the survivors of the ships they sank. But not all merchant ships sailed in convoys. In the first 18 months of World War II there were hundreds of ships, caught in various parts of the world by the outbreak of war, which had no choice but to sail for home on their own. Such lone-sailing ships were the U-boats' easiest prey, for they sailed without warship escort to pose any danger to attacking U-boats.

When a U-boat sighted a lone merchant ship, the usual course of action was to surface and invite the merchant ship's captain to surrender – after ordering him not to send any warning signals. This gave the merchant ship captain the chance to get all his crew safely into the lifeboats without any needless loss of life. Once this had been done, the U-boat would sink the ship – whenever possible with gunfire aimed at the ship's waterline, to save torpedoes.

The most considerate U-boat captains would then approach the survivors in their lifeboats and inform them exactly where they were, advising the best course to steer to reach the nearest land. If any of the survivors were injured, the U-boat captain would order first aid to be given by his own crew. He would often offer further help with regard to food and water. If the lifeboat supplies happened to include a bottle of whiskey, the U-boat captain might well offer to exchange it for a bottle of German *schnapps*!

Such fair treatment of survivors was always a good idea, for there was always the chance that a survivor might tell the U-boat captain information such as the position of the nearest British warship.

Though it was the job of the U-boats to sink as many British and American ships as they could, U-boat sailors usually felt a deep sympathy for the crews of the ships they sank. Nobody knew better than the U-boat men that they themselves could be the survivors of tomorrow.

Despite this feeling of fellowship, however, the first duty of any U-boat captain was the safety of his own ship and crew. If a merchant ship captain disobeyed the order not to send radio signals, the U-boat captain's immediate response would be to open fire on the ship, trying to destroy the radio room before the distress signal could be completed. On one occasion, a very brave radio operator kept signaling until the U-boat's shells killed him. The U-boat captain ordered his men to stand in salute in memory of a brave enemy.

▷ Survivors in life rafts and life jackets are hauled alongside a U-boat as their merchant ship goes down. U-boat crewmen prepare to offer food, water, medical treatment to the injured – and finally their position and sailing directions.

▷ Another encounter between merchant ship survivors and the crew of the U-boat which sank their ship. It was commonplace for the U-boat men to give survivors all the help they could, as between fellow-seamen.

Defeat of the U-boats

The Battle of the Atlantic reached its climax in the spring of 1943. By this date, the Germans had been mass-producing U-boats for the past 18 months, and there were more of them at sea than at any time since the war began. During the "Happy Time" of October 1940, Dönitz had had only 27 U-boats fit for sea. By March 1943 he had 240 of them, and it seemed at last that there were enough U-boats to overwhelm the convoy escorts and win total victory on the North Atlantic convoy route.

The whole outcome of the war depended on this, because by 1943 the British and American Allies were building up the huge army which would invade and free German-held Europe. If the U-boats won in the North Atlantic, the invasion of Europe could never take place. And for a few tense weeks it seemed that nothing could be done to stop the savagery of the mass U-boat attacks in the North Atlantic.

For the Allies, March 1943 was the worst-ever month of the U-boat war. U-boat attacks in the North Atlantic sank no less than 82 ships (total 476,349 tons). British Prime Minister Winston Churchill told American President Franklin D. Roosevelt that "Our escorts are everywhere too thin, and the strain upon the British Navy is becoming intolerable." The American Navy, its hands full with the Japanese war in the Pacific, had few

ships to spare for the Battle of the Atlantic.

But it was not the end. Just in time, the Allies were about to bring together all the methods of fighting U-boats which they had learned so painfully during the long, 3½-year battle. They now had **hunting groups** of new escort warships, trained to work as a team in hunting down and sinking U-boats, and they now had long-range aircraft to cover the passage of convoys across the Atlantic.

▷ May 1943, and a U-boat retreating empty-handed from a heavily defended Atlantic convoy comes under attack from rocket-firing aircraft launched from an escort carrier. In the background a surface hunting group, homed to the scene by reports from the aircraft races in to make certain of a kill.

In the convoy battles of May 1943 no less than 41 U-boats were sunk, bringing the total of U-boats lost since January up to 96. By the end of May 1943, Dönitz had had to order his surviving U-boats to withdraw from the North Atlantic. The Allies had won the Battle of the Atlantic – and, in time, the war.

During World War II, Germany brought 1,162 new U-boats into service, of which no less than 785 were destroyed.

Glossary

Asdic   British word for sonar. It was short for the British and French "Allied Submarine Detection Investigation Committee" which discovered the sonar technique between the World Wars.

Ballast tanks   The chambers in a submarine's outer shell which are flooded to dive and emptied to surface. When these tanks were "blown," the water was pumped out to be replaced by air, causing the craft to rise toward the surface.

▽ The most important feature of the Atlantic battlefield was the so-called Black Gap in mid-ocean, which early convoys had to cross with few, if any, escorts. Once the Gap was closed with long-range aircraft and surface escorts, the defeat of the U-boats was certain.

Conning tower   Small compartment within the pressure hull situated above the control room. When submerged the captain would conduct an attack from here.

Control room   Chamber inside the pressure hull from which the submarine is controlled when submerged.

Convoy   Group of merchant ships sailing in close formation for defense against enemy attack.

Depth-charge   Anti-submarine bomb, set to explode at a choice of depths.

Fix   Accurate measurement from the sun or stars, used to establish a ship's true position.

"Closing the Black Gap"

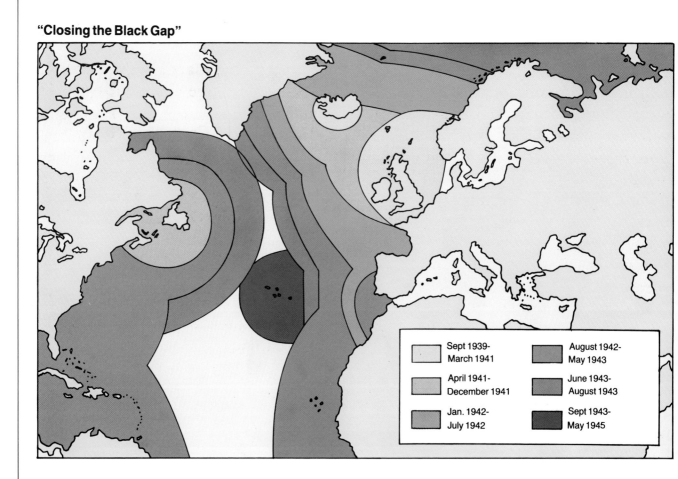

	Sept 1939–March 1941		August 1942–May 1943
	April 1941–December 1941		June 1943–August 1943
	Jan. 1942–July 1942		Sept 1943–May 1945

Timechart

Hedgehog Anti-submarine mortar which threw a pattern of 24 bombs, all fused to explode on hitting a U-boat.

Hunting group Team of surface warships trained to work closely together in tracking down and destroying U-boats.

Hydrophone Instrument for detecting enemy ships or submarines by picking up the sounds made by their engines or propellors.

Leigh light Powerful searchlight mounted in aircraft for lighting up U-boats running on the surface at night.

Pens Specially-built U-boat bases, made bomb-proof by massive upper layers of concrete.

Periscope Long viewing-tube which can be raised and lowered to see objects above the surface of the sea.

Pressure hull The strengthened inner hull of a submarine, built to withstand water pressure, containing the submarine's working and living areas.

Sonar Short for "Sound Navigation and Ranging" (known to the British as Asdic). It works by emitting an underwater "ping" which sends back an echo if a submarine is detected.

Squid Anti-submarine mortar firing a spread of three bombs.

Torpedo Main submarine weapon: self-propelled missile fired by compressed air from a tube, designed to sink ships by exploding below the waterline.

Wolf pack British and American term for the group attacks on convoys made by U-boats.

September 3, 1939 War between Britain and Germany. Total U-boat strength 57.

September 1939 – March 1940 Atlantic U-boats sink 148 merchant ships (678,130 tons).

August 1940 – March 1941 Atlantic U-boats sink 343 merchant ships (1,847,105 tons).

December 1941 War between United States and Germany extends U-boat attacks to American coast.

January 1, 1942 Total U-boat strength 91.

January – August 1942 Atlantic U-boats sink 681 merchant ships (3,544,602 tons).

January 1, 1943 Total U-boat strength 212.

January – February 1943 Atlantic U-boats sink 123 merchant ships (664,421 tons).

March 1943 Crisis of Atlantic battle. Atlantic U-boats sink 120 merchant ships (693,389 tons) in one month.

May 1943 Atlantic U-boats sink 58 merchant ships (299,428 tons), but 41 U-boats are sunk.

May 24, 1943 Surviving U-boats are withdrawn from North Atlantic.

May 1945 Surviving U-boats – 377 out of 1,174 commissioned – surrender or are scuttled.

Index